"With transparency and warmth, *Lamenting Racism* combines an uncomfortable practice with an uncomfortable subject. Working through this series is more than education: it impacts the heart and results in creativity to courageously move into next steps of racial healing. A powerful tool."
—**JO ANNE LYON**, ambassador of The Wesleyan Church

"*Lamenting Racism* calls us to sit in the dust and lament with those who are suffering the institutional sins of racism. This six-part series helps the faith community reclaim lament with the hope of turning tears of pain caused by racism into tears of joy for hearing each other."
—**MIGUEL DE LA TORRE**, professor of social ethics and Latinx studies at Iliff School of Theology

"*Lamenting Racism* offers a 'how to' for teaching and learning about racism. It pulls you right into the hard realities of racial bias in church history, biblical interpretation, mission, and life itself. A hopeful way forward through the emotion-laden, heart-rending gift of lament."
—**JAMES E. BRENNEMAN**, president of American Baptist Seminary of the West

"*Lamenting Racism* is a remarkable and helpful resource. It stands out for its invitational tone and personal approach to a difficult issue. This dynamic study places real-life stories alongside the often overlooked resource of biblical lament, creating a relatable resource for small groups and congregations that is disarming, eye-opening, and powerfully prophetic."
—**TIMOTHY R. GAINES**, associate professor of religion at Trevecca Nazarene University

"*Lamenting Racism* is a relevant, powerful, and timely resource that will engage participants and inspire hope for all. This resource provides an invitation to join the fight for justice and equality in a way that is meaningful and collaborative."
—**EDGAR BARRON**, chair and assistant professor of leadership and organizational psychology at Azusa Pacific University

"*Lamenting Racism* is a timely and accessible resource for congregations that see anti-racism as a call to discipleship. Whether your eyes have just been opened to the urgency of anti-racism work or you have been on the long and hard road for many years, *Lamenting Racism* offers a welcoming seat in the circle to cry out, repent, and let your voices be heard to the One who hears and acts with and for us."
—**SUE PARK-HUR**, denominational minister of transformation for Mennonite Church USA

"Lament moves us in the direction of telling the truth. *Lamenting Racism* leads you into this powerful practice for the sake of justice. From the psalmist's 'Hear my cry' to Marvin Gaye's 'What's goin' on,' lament is what we do when we believe that there is a God who hears us, sees us, and cares about us. All of us."
—**REGGIE L. WILLIAMS**, associate professor of Christian ethics at McCormick Theological Seminary

"The solid biblical and cultural perspectives presented by pastors and professors along with gripping real-life experiences combine to make *Lamenting Racism* a powerful teaching tool. This video resource is an excellent opportunity to see racism and lament as we may have never seen them before."
—**MATT WHITEHEAD**, bishop of the Free Methodist Church, USA

"Gleaning from their racial identity, lived experiences, and biblical research, Rob Muthiah and partnering pastors and theologians present lament as a sacred avenue to express authentic feelings of grief, anger, frustration, shame, and repentance to God in the face of racism. Compelling and timely, *Lamenting Racism* provides biblical wisdom, resources, and strategies to cultivate conversation, bolster engagement, and facilitate transformation."
—**KEITH E. HALL**, vice president and chief diversity officer at Azusa Pacific University

LAMENTING RACISM

A Christian Response
to Racial Injustice

LEADER'S GUIDE

Rob Muthiah

with Abigail Gaines, Dave Johnson,
Tamala Kelly, Brian Lugioyo, Anthony Powell,
John Ragsdale, Jessica Wai-Fong Wong

Harrisonburg, Virginia

Herald Press
PO Box 866, Harrisonburg, Virginia 22803
www.HeraldPress.com

Study guides are available for many Herald Press titles at
www.HeraldPress.com.

LAMENTING RACISM: LEADER'S GUIDE
© 2021 by Herald Press, Harrisonburg, Virginia 22803. 800-245-7894.
   All rights reserved.
Library of Congress Control Number: 2020950354
International Standard Book Number: 978-1-5138-0864-2 (paperback);
   978-1-5138-0865-9 (ebook)
Printed in United States of America
Cover and interior design by Merrill Miller

All rights reserved. This publication may not be reproduced, stored in a retrieval system, or transmitted in whole or in part, in any form, by any means, electronic, mechanical, photocopying, recording or otherwise without prior permission of the copyright owners.

This study series was produced with grant support from the Louisville Institute.

Unless otherwise noted, Scripture text is quoted from the *COMMON ENGLISH BIBLE*. Copyright © 2011 COMMON ENGLISH BIBLE. All rights reserved. Used by permission. (www.CommonEnglishBible.com).

Scripture quotations marked (NRSV) are from the *New Revised Standard Version*, © 1989, Division of Christian Education of the National Council of Churches of Christ in the United States of America. Used by permission. All rights reserved.

25 24 23 22 21   10 9 8 7 6 5 4 3 2 1

Contents

Leader's Guide Introduction.............................. 7

1. **Voicing Pain and Rage:** Confronting Racism with Lament 11
2. **The Air We Breathe:** Understanding Racism's Persuasive Power... 19
3. **God on Racism:** Knowing What the Bible Says 24
4. **Can You Hear Me?** Listening to Race-Inflected Stories...... 29
5. **It's Getting Personal:** Voicing Our Own Laments 33
6. **We've Only Just Begun:** Imagining Our Way Forward 41

Resources... 45
The Authors 49
Additional Journaling Pages 51

Leader's Guide Introduction

Thank you for your willingness to lead a group through these six sessions! We have laid out this leader's guide so that, with just a little preparation, you should be well-prepared to facilitate the session. Your role is to guide the group through each session, using the structure provided. You are not expected to be an expert on the content!

SESSION STRUCTURE

Each session has four sections:

1. Nurturing Community
2. Digging In
3. Chewing On It
4. Closing Prayer

Each *Nurturing Community* section includes introductory comments, questions to help the group begin their conversation, a challenge statement, and an opening prayer. In the *Digging In* section, your group will watch the teaching video for the session. In some sessions, additional content is included as well. The *Chewing On It* section is designed to help your group process what they are learning. The discussion questions included in this section invite participants to share their perspectives and talk about what they're thinking and feeling. This section also includes something we think is crucial: journaling—we'll elaborate on that below. The final section for each session is the *Closing Prayer*. Each of the prayers provided is taken from a lament psalm, reinforcing the understanding that the practice of lament flows from our Holy Scriptures.

ADVANCED PREPARATION

1. Make sure each participant has a copy of the participant journal.

2. Review the session in your leader's guide.

3. Test your audiovisual equipment for playing the teaching video.

4. If meeting in person, have extra pens on hand—someone will always forget!

FOR GROUPS MEETING ONLINE

All the sessions can be conducted online if your group is meeting via videoconferencing. The closing prayer will work best read in unison with only the leader unmuted rather than trying to read it responsively as printed. Part of session 5 also takes some extra thought to carry out online—you'll find an extra set of instructions related to leading that session online when you get there.

TIPS FOR GETTING THE MOST OUT OF THIS STUDY:

1. Each participant will need a hard copy of the participant journal. In addition to the printed material contained in the journal, space is provided for participants to take notes and journal in response to each session. At the end of the study, participants will each have a set of important resources as well as a compilation of their own thoughts to take with them.

2. We want to emphasize the importance of handwritten journaling as part of the learning process used in this study. We have two main reasons for incorporating journal writing:

a. Educational research has shown that writing notes by hand engages the brain differently and embeds ideas more permanently than taking notes electronically. Some participants may resist, especially if they can type a lot faster than they can write by hand. However, the slower pace of writing by hand and the physiological hand-brain connection involved contribute differently to the learning process.

b. Writing also allows for an additional way of processing. While some learn best by processing externally, others prefer to process internally before sharing their thoughts with others. The design of this study series includes both approaches as part of our attempt to connect with a range of learning styles.

Part of your role as the facilitator is to make sure the journal writing time doesn't get pushed out by other parts of the session. To encourage your group members to embrace it, you might share the reasons listed above. As a reminder, the journal writing exercises require that each person in the group have a hard copy of the participant journal to write in.

3. The leader's guide includes leader's notes. These comments, which are not included in the participant journal, appear as italicized notes within brackets, like this example: [*included in journal*]. These leader's notes indicate that the text that follows in the leader's guide is also included in the participant journal so that you can point participants to it.

4. When you come to sections labeled "Reader," you might invite someone else in the group to read those sections, or if it seems more appropriate at that moment, you might choose to read a given "Reader" section yourself.

5. We invite you to consciously engage as a participant in addition to being the facilitator.

6. Specific suggestions for facilitating:

    a. You might choose to set the tone by being the first to respond to the Nurturing Community questions, while others formulate their responses.

    b. Especially if you are meeting in an online format, we suggest that you call on each person in the group to respond to the Nurturing Community questions, while also offering participants the option to pass if they'd prefer. This will get the conversation rolling more quickly.

    c. If one person begins to dominate the conversation during the Chewing On It section, gently ask if any of the group members who haven't yet spoken have ideas they'd be willing to share.

Thank you for being willing to take on the facilitator role in this anti-racism study. We hope that the teaching videos combined with the intentional design of the discussion material will provide a powerful experience for you and your group. We pray that the Spirit will use this experience to change you and to use you in the hard work yet to be done in confronting racism and living into the fullness of God's kingdom, where the dignity of all races is a given.

Grace and peace,

—*Rob Muthiah, team lead and professor of practical theology at Azusa Pacific Seminary, with Abigail Gaines, Dave Johnson, Tamala Kelly, Brian Lugioyo, Anthony Powell, John Ragsdale, and Jessica Wai-Fong Wong*

1

Voicing Pain and Rage
Confronting Racism with Lament

NURTURING COMMUNITY

WELCOME

Leader: [*read aloud*] Thanks for joining us for this series. The goal of this six-session study is to equip us to engage the biblical practice of lament as part of our Christian calling to confront racism.

In this first session, we'll weave in some preliminary discussion questions related to race and racism, but our main focus will be on learning about biblical lament. As we come to understand and practice lament, we'll see more clearly why it matters in relation to racism.

In future sessions, we'll do additional Bible study, analyze ways racism plays out in the church and in the broader culture, and listen to personal stories from some who have suffered from racism. Then we'll draw on what we've learned to create our own laments in response to racism. In our final session, we'll initiate next steps in the struggle against racism.

WARM-UP QUESTIONS

Leader: [*If needed, have participants introduce themselves. Then ask these questions, which are included in the participant journals.*]

1. What is your earliest memory of meeting a person from a different racial background than your own?
2. What is one word that comes to mind when you hear the word *racism*?
3. What do you think of when you hear the word *lament*?

CHALLENGE

Reader: [*included in journals*] Too often, racial differences are assigned values that reflect racism. Many people of color in the broader culture, and within the church as well, continue to experience the devastating effects of racism today. Others, in the broader culture and within the church as well, unknowingly or knowingly perpetuate and benefit from racism. Racism is an evil that touches all our lives one way or another. Will the church have the courage and commitment to engage the struggle to undo the sin of racism?

OPENING PRAYER

Reader: [*included in journals*] God of creation, we praise you for making us in your image. When we fix our eyes on you, we see more clearly who we are truly called to be. May your vision of our shared identity give us the courage and determination to confront the ways we are divided and harmed by racism. As we begin this study series together, open our hearts and minds to what you would have us learn, how you would have us change, and what you would have us do. In the name of Christ we pray. Amen.

DIGGING IN

Play session 1 video

EXAMPLES OF BIBLICAL LAMENTS: [*INCLUDED IN JOURNALS*]

Individual

"Why did you let me emerge from the womb?
 I wish I had died without any eye seeing me.
Then I would be just as if I hadn't existed,
 taken from the belly to the grave" (Job 10:18-19).

Communal

"We have sinned and done wrong. We have brought guilt on ourselves and rebelled, ignoring your commands and your laws" (Daniel 9:5).

Repentance

"Have mercy on me, God, according to your faithful love!
 Wipe away my wrongdoings according to your great compassion!
Wash me completely clean of my guilt;
 purify me from my sin!" (Psalm 51:1-2).

Accusation

"You've made us a joke to all our neighbors;
 we're mocked and ridiculed by everyone around us.
You've made us a bad joke to the nations,
 something to be laughed at by all peoples" (Psalm 44:13-14).

Abandonment

"My God! My God,
 why have you left me all alone?
 Why are you so far from saving me—
  so far from my anguished groans?

My God, I cry out during the day,
>   but you don't answer;
>   even at nighttime I don't stop" (Psalm 22:1-2).

Despair

"Because of all these things I'm crying. My eyes, my own eyes pour water because a comforter who might encourage me is nowhere near. My children are destroyed because the enemy was so strong" (Lamentations 1:16).

Fear

"My soul also is struck with terror, while you, O LORD—how long?" (Psalm 6:3 NRSV).

Protest

"Why do you stand so far away, LORD,
>   hiding yourself in troubling times?" (Psalm 10:1).

"As protest, Israel's lament calls on God to account for the way things are wrong in the world, and demands that God listen and respond—to set right what is wrong, mend what is broken, and bring light to the darkness—just as it is God's essential character to do so. God is a God of mercy: let there be mercy! God is a God of justice: let there be judgment on the enemy and the evildoer! When Israel laments, it is God's faithfulness to God's promises that are at stake."

> —**REBEKAH ECKLUND**, assistant professor of theology at Loyola University Maryland

Your notes on the teaching video: [*included in journals*]

EXAMINING SCRIPTURE

Leader: In groups of two or three, follow the guidelines in your journals as you look for the lament pattern in the psalm provided.

[*Included in journals*]

Look at Psalm 6, included below.

- Which of the lament themes that were described in the teaching video (repentance, accusation, abandonment, despair, fear, or protest) appear in this psalm?
- To what extent does this psalm include these common elements of lament psalms?

    1. Direct address of God
    2. Naming realities (remembering what has happened and describing the current situation)
    3. Appeal for specific action, interventions, or justice, sometimes in the form of a question
    4. Concluding affirmation of faith, such as an expression of praise or a promise to trust God

Psalm 6

¹ Please, Lord,
   don't punish me when you are angry;
   don't discipline me when you are furious.
² Have mercy on me, Lord,
   because I'm frail.
Heal me, Lord,
   because my bones are shaking in terror!
³ My whole body is completely terrified!
      But you, Lord! How long will this last?
⁴ Come back to me, Lord! Deliver me!
   Save me for the sake of your faithful love!
⁵ No one is going to praise you
   when they are dead.
Who gives you thanks
   from the grave?

⁶ I'm worn out from groaning.
   Every night, I drench my bed with tears;
   I soak my couch all the way through.
⁷ My vision fails because of my grief;
   it's weak because of all my distress.
⁸ Get away from me, all you evildoers,
   because the Lord has heard me crying!
⁹ The Lord has listened to my request.
   The Lord accepts my prayer.
¹⁰ All my enemies will be ashamed
   and completely terrified;
   they will be defeated
   and ashamed instantly.

CHEWING ON IT
DISCUSSION QUESTIONS [*INCLUDED IN JOURNALS*]

1. What messages have you received about whether or not it is acceptable to question God, get mad at God, or protest to God? If those messages differ from what is communicated by these examples of lament in Scripture, why do you think that is?

2. As you think about lamenting racism, which lament theme or themes could you imagine using in light of your own racial story or social location?

3. How might lamenting racism look different for someone of a different racial group from you?

JOURNALING

Leader: I'd like to invite you to take a few minutes now to journal about this question: What was most important for you about the video teaching and other aspects of our time together today? [*Allow five minutes for written reflection in journals.*]

Session 1 journal entry:

The biblical basis for lament — the story by Powell in the flower shop — emotions — how to handle them. Lament gives him a resource to resolve hurts, disappointment, and anger. How do I as a white person use lament? What do I repent from?

Leader: [*when time is up*] If you need more time, I invite you to continue journaling later. If you're willing to share, what are some of the highlights from your journaling?

CLOSING PRAYER

[*Based on what fits with your own tradition, decide whether to offer an extemporaneous closing prayer or to pray together the psalm of lament offered here. If you choose to pray the psalm together, instructions are provided below.*]

Leader: [*Divide the group in two; the prayer is included in the participant journals.*] Group 1 will read the bold sections and group 2 will read the non-bold sections. We'll all join together in reading the last stanza. If the prayer doesn't describe your specific circumstances, pray it on behalf of someone else. Let's pray together this psalm of lament.

Psalm 25 (selected and adapted verses)

I offer my life to you, Lord.
My God, I trust you.

> Please don't let me be put to shame!
> Don't let my enemies rejoice over me!

For that matter, don't let anyone who hopes in you be put to shame; instead, let those who are treacherous without excuse be put to shame.

> Turn to me, God, and have mercy on me because I'm alone and suffering. My heart's troubles keep getting bigger—set me free from my distress!

Look at my suffering and trouble! Please protect my life! Deliver me! Don't let me be put to shame because I take refuge in you.

All: Let integrity and virtue guard me because I hope in you. Amen.

2

The Air We Breathe
Understanding Racism's Persuasive Power

[handwritten notes: - status additional books / - payment / 5 min.]

NURTURING COMMUNITY

WELCOME

Leader: [*read aloud*] Thanks for joining us for session 2 in this series! In the last session, we focused on what biblical lament looks like and we learned that lament includes crying out to God to express our pain, fear, repentance, protest, and suffering. Lament can be an important tool in the church's anti-racism toolbox. For lament to serve us in this way, we need to take a deeper look at the history of racism and its current realities. That's our task in this session. Please turn in your participant journal to session 2 as we get started with a couple of warm up questions.

WARM-UP QUESTIONS *[6 min.]*

Leader: [*included in journals*]

1. How would you describe your racial background?
2. On a conscious level, how big of a factor has your racial background been for you in understanding who you are?

CHALLENGE — 2 min.

Reader: [included in journals] I'm sure we'd all agree that treating others as superior or inferior because of their race is wrong. But what if we ourselves, regardless of race, are infected by this way of seeing without even knowing it? How would you find out? And if you knew, what would you do?

OPENING PRAYER

Reader: [included in journals] Loving God, you invite all people—of every ethnicity, race, and nationality—to feast together at your banquet table. But we are divided up and separated in ways that you never intended. Give us the eyes to see how this happened and how it continues to happen today. Use our time together now to help us understand more deeply the work you call us to in undoing racism. In Jesus' name we pray. Amen.

DIGGING IN — 20 min.

Play session 2 video

Your notes on the teaching video: [included in journals]

CHEWING ON IT *20 min*

DISCUSSION QUESTIONS [*INCLUDED IN JOURNALS*]

1. Can you think of examples, in addition to those given in the teaching video, of subtle or obvious ways that the dominant culture forms people to think that "white" skin is better and more desirable than darker skin?

2. The teaching video asserts that people of all races have internalized a racialized way of seeing the world. Are there ways you can identify that you yourself have internalized a racialized way of assigning value to people?

3. Do you see yourself as experiencing privilege or limits in connection to your racial background? If so, to what degree?

JOURNALING

Leader: I'd like to invite you to take a few minutes now to journal about this question: What was most important for you about the teaching and other aspects of our time together today? [*Allow five minutes for written reflection in journals.*]

Session 2 journal entry: *5 min*

22 / LAMENTING RACISM: LEADER'S GUIDE

Leader: [*when time is up*] If you need more time, I invite you to continue journaling later. If you're willing to share, what are some of the highlights from your journaling?

CLOSING PRAYER   2 min.

[*Based on what fits with your own tradition, decide whether to offer an extemporaneous closing prayer or to pray together the psalm of lament offered here. If you choose to pray the psalm together, instructions are provided below.*]

Leader: [*Divide the group in two; the prayer is included in the participant journals.*] Group 1 will read the bold sections and group 2 will read the non-bold sections. We'll all join together in reading the last stanza. If the prayer doesn't describe your specific circumstances, pray it on behalf of someone else. Let's pray together this psalm of lament.

Psalm 10 (selected and adapted verses)

Why do you stand so far away, LORD, hiding yourself in troubling times?

> Meanwhile, the wicked are proudly in hot pursuit of those who suffer.

Let them get caught in the very same schemes they've thought up!

> Their mouths are filled with curses, dishonesty, violence. Under their tongues lie troublemaking and wrongdoing.

They wait in a place perfect for ambush; from their hiding places they kill innocent people; their eyes spot those who are helpless.

> Their helpless victims are crushed; they collapse, falling prey to the strength of the wicked.

Get up, LORD! Get your fist ready, God!

Don't forget the ones who suffer!

*All: L*ORD*, you listen to the desires of those who suffer. You steady their hearts; you listen closely to them, to establish justice for the orphan and the oppressed, so that people of the land will never again be terrified. Amen.*

3

God on Racism
Knowing What the Bible Says

NURTURING COMMUNITY

WELCOME

Leader: [*read aloud*] Thanks for being here for session 3 in our six-part series on lamenting racism! Can someone remind us of something that we covered in session 1? [*Session 1 theme: biblical lament.*] How about session 2? [*Session 2 theme: how our culture indoctrinates us into racialized ways of seeing and assigning value.*] In this session, we're going to dive into what the Bible has to say related to racism. And we're also going to see how the church has often failed to live into the biblical vision.

WARM-UP QUESTIONS

Leader: [*included in journals*]
1. When you were growing up, how diverse were your school, church, or other organizations or clubs you were involved in? Do you think those experiences have shaped you positively, negatively, or some combination of both?

2. If you grew up in the church, what, if anything, did you learn there about the church's history internationally, nationally, and locally in relation to racism?

CHALLENGE

Reader: [*included in journals*] Our culture seeks to baptize each of us into a racialized identity that divides and dehumanizes. But the Bible has a different vision for our life together. Will we let ourselves be more formed by Scripture and the Holy Spirit or by the dominant messages of our culture?

OPENING PRAYER

Reader: [*included in journals*] Holy God, the Bible tells us in the book of Ephesians that you desire for dividing walls of hostility to be torn down and for new communities in your body to be built up. But our churches too often reinforce walls that separate us instead of joining your work of tearing those walls down. Convict our hearts of this, Lord, and lead us to confess our sins. Lead us to a deeper understanding and celebration of your diverse community so that we might better work out our salvation together. In the name of your Son, Jesus, we pray. Amen.

DIGGING IN

Play session 3 video

Your notes on the teaching video: [*included in journals*]

26 / LAMENTING RACISM: LEADER'S GUIDE

CHEWING ON IT

DISCUSSION QUESTIONS [*INCLUDED IN JOURNALS*]

1. What parts of the biblical narrative explored in the teaching video were new or most important to you?
2. Why do you think there has been such a big gap between the biblical vision that rules out racism and the racist history of the church?
3. In light of what you heard today, what might you want to say to God in lament, and what lament type (see session 1 for types of lament) would you choose?
4. What do you think it will take for the church nationally, your local church, and you personally to rise to the challenge set forth in today's teaching video to live into the gospel's counter-narrative, which confronts racism?

JOURNALING

Leader: I'd like to invite you to take a few minutes now to journal about this question: What was most important for you about today's teaching video and other aspects of our time together today? [*Allow five minutes for written reflection in journals.*]

Session 3 journal entry:

Leader: [*when time is up*] If you need more time, I invite you to continue journaling later. If you're willing to share, what are some of the highlights from your journaling?

CLOSING PRAYER

[*Based on what fits with your own tradition, decide whether to offer an extemporaneous closing prayer or to pray together the psalm of lament offered here. If you choose to pray the psalm together, instructions are provided below.*]

Leader: [*Divide the group in two; the prayer is included in the participant journals.*] Group 1 will read the bold sections and group 2 will read the non-bold sections. We'll all join together in reading the last stanza. If the prayer doesn't describe your specific circumstances, pray it on behalf of someone else. Let's pray together this psalm of lament.

Psalm 44 (selected and adapted verses)

We glory in God at all times and give thanks to your name forever.

> But now you've rejected and humiliated us. You've handed us over like sheep for butchering; you've scattered us among the nations.

You've sold your people for nothing, not even bothering to set a decent price. You've made us a joke to all our neighbors; we're mocked and ridiculed by everyone around us.

> Our hearts haven't turned away, neither have our steps strayed from your way. But you've crushed us in the place where jackals live, covering us with deepest darkness.

Wake up! Why are you sleeping, Lord? Get up! Don't reject us forever!

Why are you hiding your face, forgetting our suffering and oppression? Look: we're going down to the dust; our stomachs are flat on the ground!

All: Stand up! Help us! Save us for the sake of your faithful love. Amen.

4

Can You Hear Me?
Listening to Race-Inflected Stories

NURTURING COMMUNITY

WELCOME

Leader: [*read aloud*] We're in the fourth session of this series, looking at lament as a way of doing anti-racist work. In the last session, we looked at some ways that racism developed and plays out in our culture today. In this session, we're going to listen to some personal stories as a way of opening ourselves up to God's transformation and motivation.

WARM-UP QUESTIONS

Leader: [*included in journals*]

1. In what ways do you fit and not fit the stereotypes of your racial background?

2. Generally speaking, how often in a week do you think about or notice something in relation to your own racial background? Someone else's racial background?

CHALLENGE

Reader: [*included in journals*] What does it mean to listen? Listening is more than receiving sound waves. Listening is opening ourselves up to the meaning of what another person is saying. When someone else is speaking, how often do you find your attention fading out as you think about what you want to say next? How often do you allow your attention to fade because you assume you already know what the other person thinks or feels? Regardless of where you locate yourself in terms of race, there is something for you in the stories of others—if you will truly listen.

OPENING PRAYER

Reader: [*included in journals*] El Shama, our God Who Listens, thank you for always inclining your ear to hear the voices of your children. Thank you that you do not turn your face away from us, but toward us. May we reflect this same compassion and kindness as we listen for the cries of the oppressed. Where there is offense, we ask for your grace. Where there is defense, we ask for your grace. Spirit of God, give us ears to hear what you are saying to the church as we seek to bear witness to your justice and healing among us. Amen.

DIGGING IN

Play session 4 video

Your notes on the teaching video: [*included in journals*]

CHEWING ON IT

DISCUSSION QUESTIONS [*INCLUDED IN JOURNALS*]

1. What emotions did you feel as you listened to these stories? What stands out to you from these stories, and why?

2. How might you connect these individual stories to bigger themes, structures, policies, or ways of seeing within our broader culture?

3. What might you want to cry out to God about in relation to these stories or other aspects of racism?

JOURNALING

Leader: I'd like to invite you to take a few minutes now to journal about this question: What was most important for you about the teaching and other aspects of our time together today? [*Allow five minutes for written reflection in journals.*]

Session 4 journal entry:

Leader: [*when time is up*] If you need more time, I invite you to continue journaling later. If you're willing to share, what are some of the highlights from your journaling?

CLOSING PRAYER

[*Based on what fits with your own tradition, decide whether to offer an extemporaneous closing prayer or to pray together the psalm of lament offered here. If you choose to pray the psalm together, instructions are provided below.*]

Leader: [*Divide the group in two; the prayer is included in the participant journals.*] Group 1 will read the bold sections and group 2 will read the non-bold sections. We'll all join together in reading the last stanza. If the prayer doesn't describe your specific circumstances, pray it on behalf of someone else. Let's pray together this psalm of lament.

Psalm 13 (adapted)

How long will you forget me, Lord? Forever?

How long will you hide your face from me?

How long will I be left to my own wits, agony filling my heart? Daily?

How long will my enemy keep defeating me?

Look at me! Answer me, Lord my God! Restore sight to my eyes!

Otherwise, I'll sleep the sleep of death, and my enemy will say, "I won!"

My foes will rejoice over my downfall.

All: But I have trusted in your faithful love. My heart will rejoice in your salvation. Yes, I will sing to the Lord because he has been good to me. Amen.

5

It's Getting Personal
Voicing Our Own Laments

Extra resources needed

☐ Space for embodied lament experience (if you are meeting in person)

☐ Signs (if you are meeting remotely; see instructions below under Digging In: Embodied Lament)

NURTURING COMMUNITY

WELCOME

Leader: [*read aloud*] Thanks for being here for session 5 in our six-part series. As we've been talking about lament as an antiracist practice, we've looked at Scripture, we've looked at some structural aspects of racism, and we've listened to some personal stories to understand more fully what we need to lament. In this session we're going to build on all the work we've done together by creating our *own* laments.

WARM-UP QUESTIONS

Leader: [*included in journals*]

1. What is your default reaction when you see an injustice? (Give us an example to illustrate your reaction.)

    a. Futility—just try to live with it

    b. Protest—boldly cry out about it

    c. Prayer—have a talk with God about it

    d. Feigned blindness—pretend it's not really there

    e. Activation—jump in to confront it

    f. Apathy—probably can't do anything about it anyway

    g. Anger—consumed with rage

    h. Denial or rationalization—it's probably not really that bad

    i. Paralysis—feel overwhelmed and immobilized

    j. Other: _____

2. Does your default reaction change depending on whether the injustice is toward you or toward someone else?

CHALLENGE

Reader: [*included in journals*] Lament is truth-telling, and lament is never comfortable. Isn't it audacious to challenge and question God? Do we really dare to prod God to act? Most of us have been taught that addressing God in this way is unacceptable. But as we've learned, Scripture teaches us otherwise. How willing is the church—and how willing are *you*—to lament?

OPENING PRAYER

Reader: [*included in journals*] Lord God, as we begin our time together, send your Holy Spirit into our midst. May we be so filled with your Spirit that we see with crystal clarity how the way of Jesus departs from the ways of this world. May your Spirit create in us a holy discomfort in light of the enduring racism in our midst. Even as you harden our resolve to confront racism, soften our hearts and prepare us to bring our pain and our longings before you. In the name of Jesus, who lamented to you from the garden and from the cross. Amen.

DIGGING IN

Play session 5 video

Your notes on the teaching video: [*included in journals*]

WRITING PERSONAL LAMENTS

Leader: We're invited now to write our own prayers of lament in relation to some aspect of racism. In your journals you'll find the common elements in lament psalms that were described in session 1, if that's helpful for you in writing your lament. I'll give us six to eight minutes and then we'll come back together and hear from anyone who is willing to share what they wrote. Let's begin. [*Included in journals*]

Common elements in lament psalms:

1. Direct address of God
2. Naming realities (remembering what has happened and describing the current situation)
3. Appeal for specific action, interventions, or justice, sometimes in the form of a question
4. Concluding affirmation of faith, such as an expression of praise or a promise to trust God

Your personal lament:

_____

_____

_____

_____

_____

_____

_____

_____

_____

_____

Leader: [*when time is up*] I'd like to invite you now to read your lament to us if you're willing. We don't expect a highly polished piece of literature—you were only given a few minutes to write! But by reading your lament to us, your personal lament becomes communal. [*Depending on time and the size of the group, you might listen to all who are willing to share or limit it to just a few.*]

EMBODIED LAMENT

Restart video now for Anthony's introduction to this next part. *[While we have encouraged you as the facilitator to also participate fully throughout, you may find it necessary to pull back from your participant role to lead this next section.]*

If you are meeting face-to-face:

[For this experience, you might choose to arrange a space that can serve as your "stage," large enough for all participants to eventually join in the movement and sound. Alternatively, you could have everyone stand and do their actions and sounds in place. Either way, try to allow enough room for those who might choose to kneel or prostrate themselves as part of their movements.]

Leader:

1. Everybody stand up and get in a line next to our "stage."
2. Choose an action and a sound to express your lament.
3. Here we go! The first person in line: come to the stage and begin!
4. Make sure the first person is doing the action and sound repetitively. Quickly add the second person, then the third, and so on until everyone, including you, is in place and all the movements and sounds are happening at once.
5. As the leader, act as a choir director, adjusting as desired, and then ask the group to do the following:
    a. get quieter
    b. get louder
    c. slow down
    d. speed up
    e. continue the action but stop the sound
    f. resume the sound but stop the action

g. have half the group stop and watch

h. have the first half resume and the second half stop and watch

i. all resume

j. stop and go back to seats

If your group is meeting remotely, here is a method you might use:

1. In advance, create signs, using a half sheet of paper for each of the instructions under #5 above.

2. Tell the group the order in which people will go, using the order in which people appear on your screen. You could also post this in the online chat.

3. Instructions for the group:

   a. Choose an action and a sound to express your lament.

   b. When I call on you, begin your sound and action and keep repeating it while I call on the next person to join in. [*Make sure everyone is unmuted and then call on the first person to begin and quickly add each successive person.*]

4. Once everyone is started, lift up, one at a time, the signs you created beforehand and hold them in front of your camera so that everyone can see the instruction. Allow a few moments before showing the next instruction. Feel free to pick and choose from the options provided—you don't have to get through all of them.

CHEWING ON IT

DISCUSSION QUESTIONS [*INCLUDED IN JOURNALS*]

1. What was it like for you to write your own lament and to listen to laments of others in your group?
2. What was the experience of bodily lament like for you?
3. Where did you feel God's presence or absence in these experiences of written and embodied lament?
4. How do you experience this as anti-racist work?

JOURNALING

Leader: I'd like to invite you to take a few minutes now to journal about this question: What was most important for you about the teaching and other aspects of our time together today? [*Allow five minutes for written reflection in journals.*]

Session 5 journal entry:

Leader: [*when time is up*] If you need more time, I invite you to continue journaling later. If you're willing to share, what are some of the highlights from your journaling?

CLOSING PRAYER

[*Based on what fits with your own tradition, decide whether to offer an extemporaneous closing prayer or to pray together the psalm of lament offered here. If you choose to pray the psalm together, instructions are provided below.*]

Leader: [*Divide the group in two; the prayer is included in the participant journals.*] Group 1 will read the bold sections and group 2 will read the non-bold sections. We'll all join together in reading the last stanza. If the prayer doesn't describe your specific circumstances, pray it on behalf of someone else. Let's pray together this psalm of lament.

Psalm 6 (selected and adapted verses)

Please, LORD, don't punish me when you are angry; don't discipline me when you are furious.

Have mercy on me, LORD, because I'm frail. Heal me, LORD, because my bones are shaking in terror!

My whole body is completely terrified! But you, LORD! How long will this last?

Come back to me, LORD! Deliver me! Save me for the sake of your faithful love!

I'm worn out from groaning. Every night, I drench my bed with tears; I soak my couch all the way through.

My vision fails because of my grief;
it's weak because of all my distress.

All: The LORD has listened to my request. The LORD accepts my prayer. Amen.

6

We've Only Just Begun
Imagining Our Way Forward

Extra resource needed

☐ Find and be prepared to watch the YouTube video of the spoken word piece "cuz he's black" by Javon Johnson.

NURTURING COMMUNITY
WELCOME

Leader: [*read aloud*] Thanks for being here for this sixth and final session in this series! We've covered a lot of ground and had some important discussions. So now what? What happens after we come to the end of this sixth session? The focus of this session is on that very question of what's next. As has been our pattern, we're going to start with a couple of warm-up questions.

WARM-UP QUESTIONS

Leader: [*included in journals*]

1. Are you more prone to act before you think or to spend so much time thinking about something that you don't take action?

2. In life in general, are you more of a sprinter or a plodder?

CHALLENGE

Reader: [*included in journals*] The call to confront racism is urgent—people are suffering every day because of racism. Yet, short of a miracle, racism won't be eradicated quickly. So as we talk in this last session about what's next, may God fill us with a sense of holy impatience to act in the present as well as a commitment to be in this for the long haul.

OPENING PRAYER

Reader: [*included in journals*] O God of all that exists, we call to you in this moment, asking for wisdom to know how to connect all we've learned so far with what we will learn in this final session. Lord, we don't just desire to master information, but we also yearn to do what you are calling us to do in this moment. Far be it from us, O Lord, to be hearers of your word only; we want to act and live in accordance with your word as well. And we long to be people who, like the psalmist, delight to do your will. Even while we acknowledge our limitations for knowing exactly what your will is at times, we are certain of this, Lord: that your will means acting justly, loving mercy, and walking humbly with you. Lead us along that path. In the name of your Son. Amen.

DIGGING IN

Play session 6 video

Your notes on the teaching video: [*included in journals*]

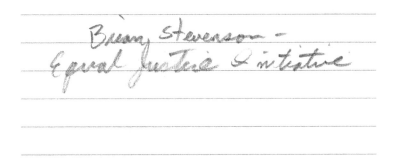

Bryan Stevenson – Equal Justice Initiative

Leader: [*after the session 6 video*] Here's a spoken word piece by Javon Johnson that is an example of what was said in the session 6 video about the arts being a way into this conversation. [*Play YouTube video of "cuz he's black" by Javon Johnson.*]

CHEWING ON IT
DISCUSSION QUESTIONS [*INCLUDED IN JOURNALS*]

1. As we come to the end of our series, what insights, learning, or convictions will you take with you? How are you challenged or changed? How does what we have discussed in this study series relate to your own spiritual journey?

2. What are some of the local, state, or national options for anti-racism work that you're most drawn to? How might you learn more about them and engage? Whom might you partner with for taking the next steps?

3. How could you share ideas from this series and ideas for next steps with your broader church family and beyond?

4. Is there anything else you'd like to share with the group as this series comes to an end?

[*For this final session, we felt it would flow best to omit journal writing, but feel free to include it if it seems helpful to you.*]

CLOSING PRAYER

[*Based on what fits with your own tradition, decide whether to offer an extemporaneous closing prayer or to pray together the psalm of lament offered here. If you choose to pray the psalm together, instructions are provided below.*]

Leader: [*Divide the group in two; the prayer is included in the participant journals.*] Group 1 will read the bold sections and group 2 will read the non-bold sections. We'll all join together in reading the last stanza. If the prayer doesn't describe your specific circumstances, pray it on behalf of someone else. Let's pray together this psalm of lament.

Psalm 86 (selected and adapted verses)

LORD, listen closely to me and answer me, because I am poor and in need. Guard my life because I am faithful.

Save your servant who trusts in you—you! My God! Have mercy on me, LORD, because I cry out to you all day long.

Make your servant's life happy again because, my Lord, I offer my life to you, because, my Lord, you are good and forgiving, full of faithful love for all those who cry out to you.

Teach me your way, LORD, so that I can walk in your truth. Make my heart focused only on honoring your name. I give thanks to you, my Lord, my God, with all my heart,

and I will glorify your name forever, because your faithful love toward me is awesome and because you've rescued my life from the lowest part of hell.

All: You, my Lord, are a God of compassion and mercy; you are very patient and full of faithful love. Amen.

Resources

BOOKS ON RACE AND RACISM

The books in this annotated list all deal with race in connection to the authors' Christian faith (we also strongly encourage you to read authors of other faiths or no faith who write on this topic). All the books listed here were written by people of color.

I'm Still Here: Black Dignity in a World Made for Whiteness by Austin Channing Brown. New York: Convergent Books, 2018.

As she traces her journey as a Black woman who grew up in predominantly white settings and has worked in predominantly white organizations, Austin Channing Brown uncovers deep racial issues present in white evangelicalism. Her compelling writing makes this one of the easiest reads on this list.

Unsettling Truths: The Ongoing, Dehumanizing Legacy of the Doctrine of Discovery by Mark Charles and Soong-Chan Rah. Downers Grove, IL: IVP, 2019.

The authors look at key historical moments related to the oppression of Native Americans and the dysfunctional theology that has been used to justify it.

Stand Your Ground: Black Bodies and the Justice of God by Kelly Brown Douglas. Maryknoll, NY: Orbis Books, 2015.

The first section of this book focuses on the history of racism, tracing how the idea of Anglo-Saxon exceptionalism developed and how that led to Black bodies being viewed as hypersexualized, dangerous, and criminal. The second section of the book is more theological.

This might be the most challenging book on this list to get through, but the effort is worth it.

Trouble I've Seen: Changing the Way the Church Views Racism by Drew G. I. Hart. Harrisonburg, VA: Herald Press, 2016.

Drew G. I. Hart draws readers in with poignant personal stories, which he weaves together with incisive analysis to uncover the broader cultural contours of racism. He blends pastoral wisdom and academic analysis to call the dominant-culture church to acknowledge and address racism.

"Letter from Birmingham Jail" by Martin Luther King Jr. Available online.

This isn't a book, but it's so good that we snuck it in. Martin Luther King Jr. wrote this letter to the white church while he sat in a Birmingham jail, under arrest for his civil rights work. Sadly, the points King made in this letter, written in 1963, are still all too relevant today.

The Color of Compromise: The Truth about the American Church's Complicity in Racism by Jemar Tisby. Grand Rapids, MI: Zondervan, 2019.

Jemar Tisby brings his training as a historian to bear as he reveals the American church's involvement in racism. His love for the church makes his critique all the more powerful.

I Bring the Voices of My People: A Womanist Vision for Racial Reconciliation by Chanequa Walker-Barnes. Grand Rapids, MI: William B. Eerdmans, 2019.

Chanequa Walker-Barnes shows the problems with many contemporary Christian attempts at racial reconciliation. As she unpacks what racism is and how it functions, she makes a particularly important contribution by showing how Black women have suffered from racism differently than Black men. She holds out hope for reconciliation, but she makes it clear that the journey toward reconciliation is much more difficult than many have assumed.

READINGS ON LAMENT

"The Costly Loss of Lament" by Walter Brueggemann, in *The Psalms and the Life of Faith*, ed. Patrick D. Miller, 98–111. Minneapolis: Fortress Press, 1998.

"With My Tears I Melt My Mattress: The Psalms of Lament" by Ellen F. Davis in *Getting Involved with God: Rediscovering the Old Testament*, 14–22. Cambridge, MA: Cowley Publications, 2001.

Jesus Wept: The Significance of Jesus' Laments in the New Testament by Rebekah Ann Eklund. New York: T & T Clark, 2015.

Lamentations and the Tears of the World by Kathleen M. O'Connor. Maryknoll, NY: Orbis Books, 2002.

Prophetic Lament: A Call for Justice in Troubled Times by Soong-Chan Rah. Downers Grove, IL: IVP Books, 2015.

"Why Me, Lord . . . Why Me? The Practice of Lament as Resistance and Deliverance" by John Swinton, in *Raging with Compassion: Pastoral Responses to the Problem of Evil*, 90–129. Grand Rapids, MI: William B. Eerdmans, 2007.

LISTENING AND LEARNING THROUGH THE ARTS

One easy way to begin listening and learning from people who don't look like you is through the poetry form of *spoken word*. The selection below includes the voices of Black and Brown artists from diverse contexts. Before you search for any of these titles on YouTube and click play, remember that your goal is to be open to the experiences of others. Put aside any temptation you might have to evaluate, judge, or disagree. Don't let the occasional rough language keep you from listening to the message of each poem. Honor others' perspectives even though they might not be yours. Be curious. What contributes to a given poet's perspective on the world? What connects with your own humanity? What might God want to reveal to you through these poems about yourself, about others, and about the world we live in?

Type a name/title into YouTube and you're on your way!

1. Alex Dang – "What Kind of Asian Are You?"
2. Crystal Valentine – "Black Privilege"

3. José Olivarez – "Mexican-American Disambiguation"
4. Rowie Shebala – "Love You Some Indians"
5. Ajanae Dawkins – "For the Blonde Girl and the Classrooms of Ghosts"
6. Manuel González – "Chicanismo"
7. Mary Black – "Quiet" (add the phrase "CBC Radio" to get the best version)
8. Lady Brion – "I Talk Black"
9. Cristina Martinez – "Chicana"
10. G Yamazawa – "10 Things You Should Know about Being an Asian from the South"
11. Anthony McPherson – "White History Month"
12. Alejandro Jimenez – "Machismo Hurts Men Too" (the spoken word piece doesn't start until the 11:00 location in the video, but his TedX talk that leads up to it is well worth a listen too!)
13. Javon Johnson – "cuz he's black" (this is the one you watched in session 6)

OTHER RESOURCES

Internet: To get started, just enter this search phrase: "how to be an anti-racist." Here's one example of a resource page with a bunch of great options: bit.ly/ANTIRACISMRESOURCES.

Podcasts: Again, an Internet search will give you lots of possibilities. Here's a favorite you might start with: *Code Switch* from NPR.

The Authors

ABIGAIL GAINES is the lead pastor of Vineyard Church Glendora and serves as the area pastor for Vineyard churches in East Los Angeles County. On any given day you will find her hanging out at the local coffee shop with her husband and their four children. It is within this context that she joins God on mission, passionately pursuing the restoration of all things. Gaines holds an MA in global leadership from Fuller Theological Seminary.

DAVE JOHNSON is the senior pastor of Neighborhood Christian Fellowship Church. He also serves as the assistant district superintendent of the Pacific Southwest District of the Wesleyan Church. Johnson has been working toward exposing and ending racism in the church for some time. He has been married for thirteen years and has three beautiful children. Johnson and his wife are passionate about foster care and adoption, and through adoption they are now raising a multiethnic family.

TAMALA KELLY and her husband, William, are the founders and lead pastors of The Purpose Church in Monrovia, California. She attended Azusa Pacific University, where she received her bachelor's, master's, and doctorate degrees. She is the founder of Empower 2 Purpose, an organization that exists to empower women to pursue their purpose with passion. She and her husband are blessed to have six children and eight grandchildren.

BRIAN LUGIOYO is a Cuban-American theologian who teaches at Azusa Pacific Seminary. His research interests are in theological anthropology and neuroscience, liturgical theology and ethics, and sixteenth-century theology, focusing on the work of Martin Bucer. He is also ordained in the Free Methodist Church.

ROB MUTHIAH teaches pastoral theology and Christian ethics at Azusa Pacific Seminary and is passionate about equipping local church leaders to pursue God's vision of justice and righteousness. He served as a pastor for a number of years and is an active member of Pasadena Mennonite Church. He is the author of *The Sabbath Experiment* and *The Priesthood of All Believers in the Twenty-First Century*.

ANTHONY POWELL is the lead pastor of Redeemed Life Church in Azusa, California. He pastors with his wife, Bonnie, and together they are parents of triplets, Lil' Anthony, Alannah, and Leilani. Powell is also a professional in the entertainment industry and a college professor in theater and dance.

JOHN RAGSDALE is an associate dean at Azusa Pacific Seminary. His academic interests are rooted in Old Testament study, though by no means does he confine himself to that area. If asked, Ragsdale will tell you he's a connector. He loves to bring people of varied interests together to solve problems and collaborate on projects. Ragsdale and his wife, Sue, have been married for forty years and have two married adult children and four wonderful grandchildren.

JESSICA WAI-FONG WONG is an associate professor of systematic theology at Azusa Pacific University and an ordained ruling elder in the Presbyterian Church (U.S.A.), where she helps lead a team focused on issues surrounding race and justice. She holds a PhD from Duke University and an MDiv from Duke Divinity School. She is the author of *(Dis)Ordered: The Holy Icon and Racial Myths*, forthcoming from Baylor University Press.

Notes

CPSIA information can be obtained
at www.ICGtesting.com
Printed in the USA
BVHW070107110121
597442BV00002B/98